The Cardiff Hill Mystery

JANET LORIMER

FEARON EDUCATION
Belmont, California

Simon & Schuster
Supplementary Education Group

The Cardiff Hill Mystery (Pacemaker)

Janet Lorimer
AR B.L.: 3.1
Points: 1.0   UG

The PACEMAKER BESTELLERS

Bestellers I

Diamonds in the Dirt
Night of the Kachina
The Verlaine Crossing
Silvabamba
The Money Game

Flight to Fear
The Time Trap
The Candy Man
Three Mile House
Dream of the Dead

Bestellers II

Black Beach
Crash Dive
Wind Over Stonehenge
Gypsy
Escape from Tomorrow

The Demeter Star
North to Oak Island
So Wild a Dream
Wet Fire
Tiger, Lion, Hawk

Bestellers III

Star Gold
Bad Moon
Jungle Jenny
Secret Spy
Little Big Top

The Animals
Counterfeit!
Night of Fire and Blood
Village of Vampires
I Died Here

Bestellers IV

Dares
Welcome to Skull Canyon
Blackbeard's Medal
Time's Reach
Trouble at Catskill Creek

The Cardiff Hill Mystery
Tomorrow's Child
Hong Kong Heat
Follow the Whales
A Changed Man

Cover and interior illustrator: Sara Boore

Copyright © 1988 by Fearon Education, 500 Harbor Boulevard, Belmont, California 94002. All rights reserved. No part of this book may be reproduced by any means, transmitted, or translated into a machine language without written permission from the publisher.

ISBN 0-8224-5340-1

Library of Congress Catalog Card Number: 87-80130

Printed in the United States of America

1. 9 8 7 6

CONTENTS

CHAPTER 1

SARAH

The telephone was ringing as Beth Calloway opened her front door. She put down the books she was carrying and ran to answer it. It was her mother, calling from San Francisco.

"Something has happened, Beth," her mother said. "Something . . ." Mrs. Calloway sounded as though she was trying not to cry.

"What's wrong?" Beth asked.

"I'm afraid I have bad news," her mother said. "It's your great-grandmother. She's had an accident. She's in the hospital."

"What happened?"

"She fell down her front steps and broke her leg. At her age that can be bad."

"I'll come at once," Beth said. "I'll fly up to San Francisco tonight."

Beth hung up the phone and then sat down to let the news sink in. Her great-grandmother, Sarah Evans, was such a wonderful woman. She was 92, but she acted younger. Sarah had always been lively. She'd lived alone for many years in a small town north of San Francisco called Stony Creek.

When Beth had been little, she'd spent her summers with Sarah. Beth loved to visit her great-grandmother. Sarah had been so good to her. She had read to her, taken her on walks, and had shown her how to knit.

As Beth grew older, her busy life got in the way of those summer visits. It had been many years since Beth had been to Stony Creek.

After Beth finished college, she'd found a teaching job at a school in Los Angeles. Now, it was almost the end of her first year of teaching. Beth had been hoping that this summer she'd be able to visit her great-grandmother.

Beth flew to San Francisco that night. Her mother picked her up and drove her to the hospital.

"I was afraid something like this would happen," Mrs. Calloway said. "She shouldn't have been living by herself. Not at her age."

"But Mom, Sarah wanted to live by herself. She wouldn't have it any other way. You know that."

"I suppose you're right, Beth."

"Can you tell me about the accident, Mom?"

"There's nothing much to tell," Mrs. Calloway said. "She fell down the front steps of her cottage. Her neighbor Lila Greene heard her cry out. Lila called the doctor and then she called us. We had Grandma brought to the hospital here in the city."

"How's she doing?" Beth said.

"Not too well," Mrs. Calloway said. "She's very weak and her mind still wanders a lot. She doesn't seem to know where she is."

"What does the doctor say?" Beth asked.

Mrs. Calloway just shook her head. Her eyes filled with tears.

When they reached Sarah's room at the hospital, Beth was quite shocked. Her great-grandmother was as white as the sheets she slept on. Sarah looked like a little rag doll lying in the big hospital bed.

Beth sat down beside the bed and took her great-grandmother's hand in her own. The older woman's skin felt cold and dry. "Sarah," Beth whispered. "Can you hear me? It's Beth."

But Sarah did not answer. Beth's eyes filled with tears. If only she could make Sarah understand that she was there.

Suddenly Sarah's eyes opened. She looked right at Beth. Her eyes seemed clear and bright. She smiled weakly.

"Beth!" she whispered.

Beth felt new hope. Maybe her great-grandmother was going to get better after all. "Sarah!" Beth said. "You know who I am."

"Of course I do. How pretty you are, Beth. I'm so glad you're here."

But Sarah's next words made no sense to Beth at all. "I hid it for you dear. It's been my secret all these years. Tom and Huck know. Ask them. They know where I hid it."

Beth frowned. "What did you hide, Sarah? What are you talking about?"

"They know," Sarah said. "Tom and Huck know. I hid it for you, dear. I hid it just for you."

Then her eyes closed again.

"Sarah!" Beth said, as if trying to call the old woman back.

Sarah did not answer.

Mrs. Calloway put her hand on her daughter's arm. "She's sleeping, Beth. Let her rest now."

"For a minute, she knew me," Beth said. "She knows I'm here, Mom. But what was she talking about?"

Mrs. Calloway shook her head. "It's nothing, I'm sure. She's old and sick. Her mind is wandering."

Both women grew still as they watched the figure in the bed. Sarah wasn't going to get better. Beth knew she'd miss her very much.

CHAPTER **2**

THE COTTAGE

Sarah died a few days later. After the funeral, Beth went back to Los Angeles. There were only three weeks left before the end of the school year. Beth was kept very busy. But she couldn't stop thinking about her great-grandmother.

Then, just before school let out, Beth got a letter from Sarah's lawyer. He'd written to say that Sarah had left everything she owned to Beth. Beth could hardly believe it. She'd been given a beautiful little house in the country! Beth remembered that the cottage was white. Red and yellow flowers grew by its fence. There was a big oak tree in the backyard. Beth had spent many happy hours swinging in an old tire that hung from that tree.

The rooms of the cottage had once seemed to Beth like those in a big doll's house. They were small and full of furniture. Sarah had liked to sit in her rocking chair in front of the fireplace. She'd spent hours there rocking and knitting.

The more Beth thought about owning the cottage, the happier she felt. She was tired from her year of teaching. She was sick of living in a crowded city. Beth decided to go up to Stony Creek as soon as she could. She would spend her summer vacation in the cottage.

Beth left Los Angeles early in the morning on a hot day in late spring. She flew to San Francisco and drove from there in her mother's car to Stony Creek. The air in the mountains was sweet and cool. And it was quiet.

"Maybe I should think about moving," Beth said to herself. "I wonder if I could get a teaching job here. It would be great to live in the country."

Stony Creek had been built during the gold rush. Its buildings were made of wood and red brick. There were big trees on either side of its main street. Stony Creek looked like a town in a movie about the Old West.

Beth had to stop at the lawyer's office to get the keys to the cottage. The lawyer was a friendly man. He told Beth the whole town was sad about Sarah's death. He hoped Beth would like being out in the country. Then he gave her two keys, one for the front door and one for the back.

Beth asked him how far it was to the cottage. "I haven't been there for a long time," she said.

"It's about five miles on the other side of town," he said. "You can't miss it. There's a white fence with a sign on it. The sign says: 'Cardiff Hill.'"

"Cardiff Hill?" Beth asked.

"That's what Sarah named her house," the lawyer answered.

"Why did she do that? Is the house on a hill by that name?"

The lawyer shook his head. "I don't really know why Sarah called her place Cardiff Hill. It always seemed strange to me. But Sarah did have some funny ways."

Beth thanked the man and went back to her car. She was glad she didn't have to do much more driving. She was very tired of sitting.

Five miles out of town Beth spotted the house on the left side of the road. She parked near the front gate. When she got out of her car, she saw a big yellow dog. The dog was tied up in the front yard. As soon as it saw Beth, it began to jump and bark.

Beth looked at the dog in surprise. She wondered who owned it and why it was in Sarah's yard. Sarah had always kept at least one cat, but she'd never owned a dog.

The closer Beth got to the gate, the more the dog barked. There was no way Beth could get into the yard. She wasn't sure what to do. Then she heard someone call, "Daisy! Down, girl!"

An old woman came hurrying from the house next door. She had white hair and was wearing a bright blue dress.

"Daisy! Stop that barking!" the woman said. The dog stopped barking and sat down. The woman turned to Beth with a smile. "I'm sorry about Daisy," she said. "But as soon as she gets to know you, she'll be your friend for life. By the way, I'm Lila Greene. And you must be Beth Calloway."

"How did you know?" Beth asked.

"From the way Sarah always talked about you." Lila's eyes began to fill with tears. "I really miss Sarah," she said sadly. "She was my best friend. We'd been neighbors for years."

Lila quickly wiped away her tears. "You look just like I thought you would my dear. In fact, you look a bit like Sarah. She used to talk about you all the time. My, you're a pretty girl."

"Thank you," Beth said. "I'm sorry Sarah's gone, too. I really miss her. I just wish I'd visited her more often."

"Well, now that you're here, I know we'll be good friends. But first things first. Let's get you moved in."

CHAPTER **3**

NEWS GETS AROUND

Lila introduced Beth to Daisy. "While you two get to know each other, I'll go get the keys to Sarah's house," Lila said.

"What keys?" Beth asked.

"Sarah gave me a set," Lila said. "She wanted me to be able to feed her cats if she was ever away."

"I see," Beth said. "But I won't need your keys, Lila. The lawyer gave me the set he had. Come on. I can't wait to see the inside of the cottage."

But even as Beth looked more closely at the outside of the cottage, her hopes began to fall. The paint was peeling. There were loose bricks in the chimney. The fence was leaning to one side. Beth hoped the inside of the cottage was in better shape.

"Is Daisy your dog?" Beth asked as they climbed the front steps.

Lila nodded. "Daisy's a good watchdog. I like to keep her in my yard. But after Sarah's house was broken into, I put her in this yard."

Beth looked at Lila in surprise. "When did that happen?" she asked.

"After Sarah's accident. When she was in the hospital, someone broke into her house."

"I didn't think a little town like this would have that kind of problem," Beth said.

"I guess no place is really safe these days," Lila said.

"But why would someone break into Sarah's house? She never owned anything really valuable, did she?"

"I think the intruder was looking for whatever Sarah hid," Lila said.

"What are you talking about?"

"Sarah hid something in her house. Something very valuable. She talked about it a lot. Everyone in town heard her."

Beth now remembered Sarah's last words. "I hid it for you, dear. I hid it just for you."

"How long had she been talking about it?" Beth asked.

"Not long," Lila said. "It started a few months ago. Of course, Sarah's mind had already started to wander. But she talked about it so much, I began to believe her."

"Oh, Lila," Beth said. "I think it was just old age. I'm sure Sarah didn't have anything valuable."

"You never know," Lila said. "Someone must have believed her story. Or why would they have broken in?"

"Maybe it was someone looking for a TV or something like that," Beth said.

"I don't know," Lila said. "I don't think so."

Lila and Beth began climbing the steps to Sarah's front door. Beth could see that Lila liked the idea of a hidden treasure in the cottage. She tried not to smile.

Just as they reached the top step, Beth caught her foot and nearly fell. She looked down to see that she'd tripped on a loose board. Beth shivered, thinking it might have been a loose board that had made Sarah fall. She decided to nail down the board as soon as possible.

When Beth got a good look at the inside of the cottage, she sighed. It was no better than the outside. There were a lot of things that needed to be fixed. A water tap dripped in the kitchen. Some of the windows were stuck. And it looked like the fireplace hadn't been used for a long, long time. Beth wondered why Sarah had let things go this way.

"There's a lot to be done to this old place," Lila said. "Sarah never got around to it. She kept saying she'd get it fixed up later."

"That's too bad," Beth said. The cottage also needed a good cleaning. There was dust everywhere. "I can see I have my work cut out for me."

"Listen," Lila said. "Why don't you come over to my house for dinner tonight? We'll have a nice meal and I'll tell you all about Sarah."

Beth smiled. "I'd like that very much."

After Lila left, Beth brought her things in from the car. She found some tools in the kitchen and nailed down the loose board. Then she began to clean the house.

While she worked, Beth did a lot of thinking. Should she keep the cottage or just sell it? It was going to take a lot of work to fix it up. It would also take a good deal of money. Was it worth it?

After she'd put clean sheets on the bed, Beth decided to take a break. She needed to buy food for the next few days. She was glad for the chance to get out of the dusty cottage for a while.

When she got to town, Beth found that the Stony Creek General Store had all the things she needed.

While she was putting her things in the car, Beth heard someone behind her. She turned and saw that a tall gray-haired man had been watching her. He introduced himself as Peter Acton. "I buy and sell houses," he said. "I know you just got here. I'd like to welcome you to Stony Creek. I was so sorry to hear about Sarah. She was a grand old lady. We'll all miss her."

"Why, thank you," Beth said. "But how do you know who I am?"

"This is a small town," Peter Acton said. "News gets around fast. Now, about that house of yours. I know you'll want to sell it as soon as possible. And I'm just the person who can help you."

Beth looked surprised. "Well," she said, "I'll let you know if I decide to sell."

"What do you mean, *if* you decide to sell?"

"Just that," Beth said. "I'll be staying in the house all summer. After that, I'll decide what to do."

"All summer? You're going to stay there all summer? That's not such a good idea, you know."

"Why not?" Beth asked.

"That house is in bad shape. Don't you think you should take a good look at it before you move in?"

"I've already seen it," Beth said. "I know it needs to be fixed up."

Peter Acton frowned. "Be careful, Miss Calloway. The way that house is, you could have a bad accident."

"Why are you so interested in the cottage?" Beth asked.

"Interested? Me? I'm just trying to be friendly, Miss Calloway. I don't want anything to happen to you." Peter Acton smiled. In Beth's eyes, the smile did nothing to make him seem less pushy. Beth turned and walked away.

CHAPTER **4**

TOM AND HUCK

When Beth got back to the cottage, there was a van parked near her gate. Lila was talking to a short bald man and a tall red-headed woman. Lila introduced them as Sam and Ruby Moore.

"We sell antiques in Stony Creek," Ruby said in a very loud voice.

"One of these days I'll have to visit your store," Beth said. "I'm very interested in antiques."

"Oh?" Ruby said. "Do you know much about them?"

"Not enough," Beth said. "I'd like to learn more."

"We just dropped by to welcome you to Stony Creek," Sam said. "We sure liked Sarah. We'll miss her."

Beth could see that Lila was trying to hide a smile. She wondered why.

Ruby poked Sam's side. "Tell her—" Ruby began.

"Okay, okay," Sam said quickly. "The other reason we stopped by was to get a look inside your cottage."

"Why?" Beth asked.

"We'd like to see the stuff you want to sell. There could be some valuable antiques in there, Miss Calloway. They could make a lot of money for you."

"Mr. Moore, I just got here," Beth said. "I haven't had time to decide what I'm going to do with my great-grandmother's things."

"There's no time like the present," Ruby said loudly. She gave Sam a push. "Well, go on. Don't just stand there, go look!"

"Hold on a minute!" Beth said. "I told you I haven't made up my mind what I'm going to do. I may not want to sell anything."

"Well, it won't hurt for Sam to take a look," Ruby said. "We can give you a good price for that old stuff."

"I thought you said there might be antiques," Beth said. "Now it's just old stuff?"

Ruby turned as red as her hair. "Look," Beth went on, "I don't have time to show you around. Maybe some other day."

Sam and Ruby didn't seem happy to hear this. "Are you really planning to stay in the cottage?" Ruby asked.

"Of course," Beth said. "Why not?"

"You don't know what might be in there," Ruby said.

"Such as?"

"Rats! The place may be full of them!" Ruby shivered as she spoke.

Beth began to laugh. She couldn't help it.

An angry look came over Ruby's face. She didn't like being laughed at.

"There's a lot of dust," Beth said, "but no rats. I didn't even see a mouse."

Ruby didn't say another word. She and Sam got into their van and drove away.

Beth shook her head. "What a pair!" she said.

"Sarah never liked them," Lila said. "And I don't think they really cared for her. That's why I almost laughed when Sam said they'd miss her. They just want to get their hands on her things."

"But why?" Beth said. "I don't think Sarah had any antiques."

"Their business isn't doing so well," Lila said. "I think they'd like to get hold of anything they can sell. I'd be careful of them."

"Don't worry," Beth said. "I will."

Beth was putting away the food she'd bought when another visitor walked in on her. But this one had four feet, not two. He acted like he belonged there. He was a big gray tomcat. He rubbed against Beth's leg in a friendly way.

Beth sat down on the floor and held out her hand. "Hello, Mr. Cat. Are you hungry?"

The cat rubbed his head against Beth's hand. "I think we're going to be friends," Beth said. "But you'll like me a lot more if I feed you."

Beth found a can of cat food in her great-grandmother's kitchen, and opened it. While the cat was eating, Beth looked at her watch. It was time for her own dinner. She left the cottage and went over to Lila's house.

Lila had fixed a good meal and Beth was very hungry. After dinner, the two talked about Sarah.

"She was my best friend," Lila said. "Sarah Evans was a great person. She was so bright and lively and fun to be with. She loved animals, you know. She always had one or two cats to keep her company."

"I know," Beth said. "In fact, one of the cats came to see me a little while ago."

"That would be Tom," Lila said. "I've been taking care of him since Sarah's accident."

"Tom?" Beth laughed. "Sarah named her tomcat Tom?"

"She named him after Tom Sawyer," Lila said. "There used to be another cat, named Huck. He was named after Huckleberry Finn. But poor old Huck died a few years ago.

"Tom Sawyer and Huckleberry Finn," Beth said. "Those were boys in books by Mark Twain."

"Of course," Lila said. "Sarah always named her cats after people in Mark Twain's books."

"My great-grandmother must have liked Mark Twain a lot," Beth said. "She read *The Adventures of Tom Sawyer* to me when I was little."

"Sarah met him once, you know."

"Really?" Beth said.

"It was back in Missouri in 1904," said Lila. "Mr. Twain was visiting his hometown. Sarah was a little girl then. Just eight years old. Her parents took her to meet him."

Beth smiled. "That must have been quite a day for her."

"Oh, it was," Lila said. "Sarah never forgot it. Mark Twain was getting old by that time. But he had always loved children. He held little Sarah on his lap. He told her she reminded him of his daughter Susy. Susy died when she was a young woman. Mr. Twain still missed her."

"To meet Mark Twain in person," Beth said. "That would be something to remember."

"Mark Twain was always Sarah's favorite writer," Lila said. "She had all his books. She even named her house after a place in one of his books."

"So that's where she got the name Cardiff Hill," Beth said. "I wondered about that."

Beth looked at her watch. "Oh, Lila, it's getting late. I really need to get some sleep. It's been a long day for me."

At Lila's front door, Beth thanked her for dinner. "I had such a good time tonight," she added.

"So did I," Lila said. "I'm very glad you're here, Beth. It's nice to have a neighbor again."

CHAPTER **5**

DAISY

As she walked back to the cottage, Beth thought about Daisy. The poor dog had been tied up all day. Maybe Daisy would like a quick run before Beth went to bed.

"Daisy," Beth called. "Here, girl!"

But the dog didn't come. Beth frowned. That was strange. She and Daisy had already become friends. Beth thought the dog would come when she called her.

"Daisy, where are you?" Beth went over to where she thought Daisy had been tied up and almost tripped over her.

"Daisy! What's wrong with you?"

The dog seemed to be sleeping. But Beth could tell that something was wrong. Daisy lay there as if she'd been drugged.

Beth looked quickly at the house. Her heart began to pound. The front door was standing wide open! Beth knew she had locked it before she'd left.

Without thinking, Beth left Daisy and ran up the front steps. In the living room she stopped. It was too dark for her to see clearly. She reached out to turn on the light. Her fingers touched something warm. Beth screamed and pulled away. It was a human arm!

Suddenly she was pushed. As Beth fell to the floor she heard the person run past her and out of the house. Before Beth could get up, she heard a car start up and drive off.

Beth was angry at herself. How could she have gone running into the house like that? Why hadn't she stopped to think? Well, it was too late now. The intruder was gone. She only hoped that Daisy would be all right and that nothing had been taken. Beth called the sheriff.

Just after Beth made the call, Lila came into the kitchen. "I heard a scream," Lila said. "Are you all right, Beth?"

Beth told Lila what had happened. "I'm worried about Daisy," she said. She and Lila went outside to check the dog.

"I think she'll be all right," Lila said. "But we should have the doctor check her."

Beth nodded. She felt sick about what had happened to Daisy. If she ever got her hands on that intruder . . .

A few minutes later, the sheriff drove up. He was a big man with a deep voice. When Beth told him her story, he shook his head. "You could have been badly hurt, Miss Calloway. You should have known better than to run into the house like that."

"I know," Beth sighed. "I feel so silly now. I just didn't stop to think."

"Is anything missing?" the sheriff asked. "Did the intruder get anything?"

"I don't know yet," Beth said.

"How's the dog?" the sheriff asked Lila.

Lila said she thought the doctor should look at Daisy. The sheriff nodded. "I can take her into town for you," he said. "As for you, Miss Calloway, I think you'd better find some place where it's safer."

"She can stay with me," Lila said. "I have lots of room."

"Thank you," Beth said, "but I wouldn't dream of leaving this place empty. I don't know what the intruder was after, but this is the second time the house has been broken into."

"Yes," the sheriff said. "That's all the more reason for you to stay with Lila."

Beth shook her head. "No way! I lived alone in Los Angeles. I'm sure I can take care of myself here, too. I'm not afraid. But what are you going to do about this, sheriff? Can't you take fingerprints or something?"

"We don't even know if the intruder had time to take anything. Why don't you call me tomorrow if you think something's missing?"

"Thanks a lot," Beth said coldly.

After Lila had gone home and the sheriff left with Daisy, Beth decided to make herself a cup of tea. She was tired, but she couldn't sleep. She had too much to think about.

While she drank her tea, Beth thought about the break-in. Sarah had very little furniture. Beth was sure none of it was valuable. Beth hadn't looked in the drawers and closets yet. But she was pretty sure that she wouldn't find much.

So why had someone tried to break in twice? Did the intruder really think there was something valuable here?

Beth thought about the people she'd met that day. Peter Acton had wanted her to sell the cottage. The Moores couldn't wait to get into it. Could one of them be behind the break-ins? What about Lila? She'd said she believed Sarah really had hidden something. But Lila had a set of keys. She didn't need to break in. She and Beth had been together when the intruder had come tonight. Or was Lila working with someone else? Had she asked Beth over just to get her out of the house?

Beth had questions but no answers. Worse, she was beginning to suspect everyone, even the sheriff. After all, he'd told Beth to leave, too.

What she needed was a good night's sleep. Maybe in the morning things would start to make sense.

CHAPTER **6**

THROWN FORWARD

When Beth awoke, she felt great. A good night's sleep had done wonders for her. It was going to be a lovely day. The sky was a clear blue, the sun a bright yellow. Birds sang in the oak tree. Beth could even smell the flowers that grew by the fence.

She got up and made breakfast. While she ate, she made plans for the day. She wanted to finish cleaning the house. She also wanted to buy new locks for the doors and see how Daisy was doing.

Beth was feeling good as she drove into town. What had happened last night seemed like only a dream now. Beth sang to herself as she drove.

The road Beth was on went down a hill just before it reached town. At the top of the hill, Beth stepped on the brake pedal to slow down. Nothing happened. She pushed the pedal to the floor. The car began to pick up speed. Beth stamped on the brake pedal again and again. She could see the crowded cross street at the foot of the hill. Beth had to stop the car before she killed herself or someone else.

She reached for the hand brake and turned the car to the right. It smashed into the bank at the side of the road. Beth was thrown forward. Her seat belt kept her from hitting her head on anything.

For a minute, she just sat there, too shaken to move. Then she heard a car pull up next to hers. A voice asked, "Are you all right, Miss Calloway?"

Beth turned and saw the sheriff. "I . . . I think so," she said weakly. The sheriff helped her out of the car.

"That's a bad hill," the sheriff said. "People are always coming down it too fast."

"But I wasn't driving fast," Beth said. "Something went wrong with my brakes."

The sheriff didn't seem to believe her. "Well, see for yourself," Beth said in an angry voice. "Why don't you check them?"

The sheriff just nodded. But after he had checked the brakes, he said, "You're right. These brake lines were cut."

"Cut! You mean it was done *on purpose?*"

"It sure looks like it," the sheriff said. "I guess someone doesn't like you, Miss Calloway."

"But I haven't been here long enough," Beth said. "People hardly know me. No, Sheriff, I think somebody wants me out of the cottage."

The sheriff pushed his hat to the back of his head. "You think this was done by your intruder?"

Beth nodded. "I'm sure of it. Someone thinks there's something hidden in the cottage. Something worth a lot of money. Sarah told people about it. I guess someone believed her."

"And you don't," the sheriff said.

Beth frowned. "I don't know," she said. "At first I didn't. I thought Lila was just talking. Now I'm not so sure."

"Well, someone believes Sarah's story," the sheriff said. "I think you should move out of there right away. Get out before something else happens to you."

"No!" Beth said. "I told you last night, I won't be frightened away. Look, you're the sheriff. Can't you post a guard or something?"

The sheriff laughed. "Miss Calloway, that's just not possible. There aren't enough people on the force. We have to cover a large area. I can't spare someone just to guard you. So why don't you be smart and move out of that place?"

The sheriff started back to his car. "Come on," he said. "I'll drive you to the service station. They can tow your car in. Maybe you can rent a car from them while yours is being fixed."

Beth climbed into the sheriff's car. She was frightened, but she was also angry. This had been no accident. Someone wanted her out of the way.

Beth then thought of her great-grandmother's fall. Was that really an accident? Or had someone pulled the board loose on purpose, so that she would trip and fall? If this were true, her great-grandmother's death had been murder.

Beth was able to rent a car at the service station. She then went to see Daisy. The dog was still weak and the doctor said Daisy needed to rest. He wanted to keep an eye on her for a few days.

Beth went to the general store to buy new locks. She decided to put them in herself that afternoon. She also decided that the sooner she searched the cottage, the better. It was time she looked for whatever her great-grandmother might have hidden.

CHAPTER 7
HIDING PLACES

When Beth reached the cottage, she saw an old blue truck parked by the gate. A man in white overalls was taking a big toolbox out of the truck.

Beth jumped out of her car and ran over to the truck. "Who are you?" she asked. She knew she sounded angry. She didn't mean to, but she couldn't help it. She was sick and tired of strangers showing up at her front gate.

The man looked at her in surprise. "The name is George Kelly, Miss Calloway."

"What do you want?" Beth asked.

"Why, I just stopped by to get to work on your chimney. I guess you can see it needs to be fixed. And the roof, too. The outside needs painting. The inside needs—"

"I know all that," Beth said quickly. "But how did you know I wanted to get the place fixed up? And how do you know who I am?"

"Why everyone knows who you are, Miss Calloway. This is a small town and the news—"

". . . gets around fast," Beth said. "Yes, so I've been told."

"Your great-grandmother called me some time ago," Kelly went on. "She asked me to stop by to fix up the place. The trouble is, I was too busy with other jobs. That's what I do, Miss Calloway. I'm Stony Creek's 'fix-it' man. I thought you'd want me to do the work for you."

"I see," Beth said.

"I told Sarah I'd stop by as soon as I could. But I'm just now getting around to it. Is something wrong?"

Beth could see that George Kelly thought she was pretty odd. By this afternoon, word would be all over town. "Beth Calloway isn't very neighborly," they'd say. "You know how city people are."

But Beth didn't know if George Kelly was telling the truth. It was very interesting that he had just now found the time to stop by the cottage. But if Kelly was handy with tools, he could have pulled up that board on Sarah's front steps. He could have cut Beth's brake lines.

Beth was reaching her breaking point. She didn't know who to trust.

"I-I'm sorry if I sounded angry," Beth said. "But this isn't a good day for you to start on the cottage. I wonder if you could come back in a few days."

Kelly thought about it for a minute. He shook his head slowly. "I don't know," he said at last. "A lot of people have been calling me. Could be I'll get another job that will last for weeks. This may be your last chance for a long time, Miss Calloway."

"I'll just have to take that chance," Beth said.

Kelly frowned and put his toolbox back in the truck. He drove away without saying another word. Beth sighed to herself. Had she been wrong to send him away? She just didn't know.

Beth looked at the cottage. It was a sweet little place. But what was its secret?

Beth walked inside and tried to see past the furniture and books. She was looking for a hiding place. She knew she would have to go over every inch of the cottage.

She began with the kitchen. Beth checked all the drawers and cupboards. She looked under the sink. She tapped on the walls, but they didn't sound hollow. She even looked for a trapdoor in the floor. There was none.

After she'd searched the kitchen, Beth went on to the other rooms. She looked in closets, drawers, and cupboards. Soon she was covered with dust.

Beth walked back to the living room. This was the last room she had to search. She looked around. There were no cupboards or closets here, just the furniture and lots of books. Beth looked at the books carefully. Maybe there was a hiding place behind them. She began to pull the books off the shelves. Before long she had piles of books on the floor, on the tables, and on the chairs. But the shelves held nothing else, and there was nothing behind the shelves.

Beth looked at the piles of books and sighed. All she was doing was making a bigger mess. She began to put the books back. Then she stopped short.

Many of the books were by Mark Twain. Could it be that the hidden thing had something to do with him? Maybe one of the books was very old. That would make it valuable. Beth looked at each book carefully. None of them were *that* old.

Beth sat down in her great-grandmother's rocker. She was hot, tired, and dusty. She'd had no luck. All of a sudden she felt very hungry. She looked at her watch. It was way past noon.

Beth made herself something to eat and took her plate of food back to the living room. She decided to read while she ate. Maybe it would take her mind off her troubles.

On the floor by the rocker was Sarah's copy of *The Adventures of Tom Sawyer*. Beth picked up the book and opened it. Almost at once she lost herself in the story.

The hours slipped by without Beth's knowing it. She was too busy reading about Tom, Huck, and Becky Thatcher.

Beth had just reached the part where Tom and Huck were hiding in the graveyard. It was the middle of the night. Someone was digging up a body.

The sudden sharp ring of the telephone made Beth jump in her seat. She looked around quickly. The late afternoon sun was almost gone. It was getting dark.

The telephone rang again. Beth went to the kitchen to answer it. "Hello?" she said.

There was a minute of silence. Then a voice said, "Get out, Beth Calloway. Get out of that cottage now! Get out before you die!"

CHAPTER **8**

"I WON'T TELL"

Before Beth could say a word, the caller hung up. Beth's heart was pounding. She backed away from the telephone. Her first thought was to run from the cottage.

Beth started for the back door, then stopped. If she left now, she would be giving in to the caller. She might never find out who it was.

Beth became angry. No one had the right to frighten her away. No, she would *not* leave. One way or another, she was going to get to the bottom of the mystery.

Beth returned to the living room. She hadn't finished searching it yet. Now she was in such a hurry that she threw things every which way.

How, Beth wondered, could she hope to find what her great-grandmother had hidden? She didn't even know what it was. Maybe Lila could give her some answers.

Beth ran back to the kitchen to call her neighbor. As she reached for the telephone she remembered that last night she had suspected Lila. Could she have been the one who'd made that frightening call?

But Lila was the only person who could help Beth now. If Lila was innocent, she would answer Beth's questions. Beth picked up the telephone.

When Lila answered, Beth said, "I've been thinking about Sarah. I can't stop wondering about what she hid in the cottage. Do you have any ideas, Lila?"

"I wish I could help you," Lila said. "But I don't think I can. Sarah didn't seem to have much money. And she didn't have any valuable jewelry."

"Maybe it was something she kept in the bank," Beth said. "You know, in a safe deposit box. Maybe an old book. That could be valuable."

"I don't think so. Your great-grandmother didn't trust banks. She didn't trust lawyers very much either. Sarah made out her will just a few months ago. That was the only time she ever went to see a lawyer."

Beth sighed. Then she had a new thought. "Did other people know that she didn't trust banks?"

"Oh, yes," Lila said. "It was no secret."

"Just when did she start to talk about that thing she hid?" Beth asked.

"Like I told you before, just a few months ago. Right after she made out her will. That's when she started acting so strange. Sometimes she would act like she was a child again. She seemed to think I was her mother. She'd say, 'I'll take good care of it, Mother. Don't you worry. I won't tell.'"

"That is strange," Beth said.

"Then there were times she thought she was talking to Mark Twain. She would thank him for being so kind to her. She'd say it would always be their secret."

"What was their secret?" Beth asked.

"I don't know," Lila said. "I never found out."

Beth thanked Lila and hung up. She was pretty sure now that Lila was innocent. But Lila didn't know much more than Beth did.

Beth thought hard about what Lila had said. People knew that Sarah didn't trust banks. But

Lila had said Sarah didn't seem to have much money, anyway. Maybe Lila was wrong. Sometimes old people hid money in strange places. Was that what Sarah had hidden? Money?

By now the sun had set. The kitchen was quite dark. Beth turned on the light. She also turned on the lights in the other rooms. It helped a little, but the cottage was too quiet. Beth was beginning to feel jumpy.

Something warm and soft touched Beth's leg. Beth let out a sharp cry and jumped back. She looked down. It was only Tom, wanting to be fed.

Beth reached down to pat him. "Oh, Tom," she sighed, "how I wish you could tell me what Sarah hid. And *where* she hid it."

Suddenly her great-grandmother's last words came back to Beth. "Ask Tom and Huck! They know where it is."

CHAPTER **9**

TREASURE

Ask the cats? That made no sense. Huck was already dead. Sarah had known that. So what had she meant?

Beth fed Tom, but she wasn't thinking about the cat. She was thinking about what her great-grandmother had said. Then she remembered the book she'd been reading. Tom Sawyer and Huckleberry Finn were in *The Adventures of Tom Sawyer*. Tom and Huck! Had Sarah meant the boys in the story? Had she hidden something in the book? Maybe there was a note, or a map, that would lead Beth to the hiding place.

Beth picked up the book again. She shook it but nothing fell out from between its pages. Maybe there was something hidden in the spine of the book. Beth got a knitting needle and worked it down into the spine. But there was nothing there either.

What had Sarah been trying to tell her? Could the answer be in the story itself? Beth turned to the table of contents. She began to read what was in each chapter. There it was! Chapter 25: "Search for the Treasure."

Beth quickly turned to that chapter. Her hands were shaking badly. She sat down in the rocking chair and began to read.

Tom and Huck had decided to hunt for buried treasure. One of the places they wanted to search was an old empty house. The house was at the bottom of Cardiff Hill.

Beth's heart was pounding now. She knew she was onto something.

Tom and Huck went into the house. People had said it was haunted. The boys were jumpy. They went up the stairs to the second floor. While they were looking around, they heard voices. Someone was coming! The boys were so frightened they could hardly move.

Two men came into the old house. They had something to hide. They decided to hide it under a stone in the fireplace. While they were digging up the stone, they found a box. It was filled with gold.

Beth looked from the book to the fireplace. Was that what Sarah had been trying to tell her? To look in the fireplace? It hadn't been used for a long time. Beth had wondered why. It seemed Sarah would have needed to heat the little cottage. But she might not have built a fire if . . .

Beth walked over to the fireplace and looked at it more closely. It was full of leaves that had come down the chimney. Beth cleaned it out. Some of the bricks on the floor of the fireplace were higher than the others. Beth used the poker to work those bricks loose. When she pulled them out, she uncovered an old metal box.

Beth lifted the box out of the fireplace. The box wasn't heavy, but it was locked. Sarah must have had a key to it. What had she done with it? The lawyer had given Beth only house keys. And Beth hadn't found any other keys when she'd searched the house.

Beth then remembered that Lila had a set of keys. Maybe she had the key to the box and didn't know what it was for. Beth decided to call her. When Lila answered the phone, Beth said, "Lila, you know the keys Sarah gave you? Is there a small key with them?"

"Let me go look," Lila said. When she came back to the telephone, Lila said, "Why yes, Beth, there is. I never knew what it was for. Do you?"

"I think so," Beth said. "Could you bring it over?"

"Right away," Lila said. She hung up.

At that moment there was a loud screech from the living room. Beth went to see what had made the sound.

She was just in time to see Ruby Moore picking up the metal box.

"Stop!" Beth shouted.

Ruby gasped and dropped the box. But then Beth saw that in her other hand Ruby was holding a gun!

Out of the corner of her eye, Beth saw what had made the screech. It was poor Tom, backed into a corner. Ruby must have stepped on him by accident.

"You can't get away with this, Ruby," Beth said.

Ruby laughed. "Oh, no? Watch me!"

"Do you know what's in the box?"

"It's something valuable," Ruby said, "and I aim to have it. It could be money. Or maybe jewelry. Who knows? But it's something that's worth a lot of money. Everyone knows Sarah Evans didn't trust banks."

Beth now saw a strange light in Ruby's eyes. The woman was a bit mad. But knowing this didn't help Beth right now.

"I have a right to it," Ruby said. "I need it. It's going to be my ticket to a new life." She frowned. "Do you think I like living in this town? Do you think I like being poor? I hate it! I hate everyone knowing what everyone else is doing!"

Beth knew she had to keep Ruby talking. Maybe she could figure a way out of this mess before Ruby killed her.

"What about Sam?" Beth asked. "Does he know what you're doing?"

"Sam!" Ruby laughed again. "Who cares about Sam? This was my idea, my plan!"

"Tell me," Beth said, "did you pull that board loose on the steps? And cut my brake lines? And break in here twice?"

Ruby waited a minute and then said loudly, "Yes!" Her eyes were shining. "Sarah talked about hiding something valuable. I had to find out what it was. I came to see her. I told her I wanted to see if she had any antiques she could sell me. She wouldn't let me in. Sarah always looked down her nose at me. But I thought of a way to get even. And it worked. She tripped over that loose board and fell. After she was taken to the hospital, I broke in. But that nosy Lila almost caught me. She tied the dog in the yard after that. Before I knew it, you showed up."

Beth felt a sudden rush of anger. Ruby had caused her great-grandmother's death. She had drugged Daisy and cut the brake lines in Beth's car. Now she might kill Beth. Ruby didn't care what she did to get that box.

Keep her talking! Beth thought to herself. Keep her talking!

"I guess you were the one who made that telephone call today," Beth said.

"Yes, yes!" Ruby said quickly. "I did it all. Pretty smart, if I do say so myself. It's too bad you didn't do what you were told, Beth Calloway. Too bad you didn't leave. But now it's too late."

"Ruby, don't!" Beth said. "If you kill me, it'll be murder. You won't get away with it."

"No one will know," Ruby laughed. "We're way out in the country. There's only old Lila next door. By the time she can do anything, I'll be long gone."

Ruby raised the gun.

CHAPTER 10

SARAH'S SECRET

Beth knew she had to act fast if she wanted to save her life. She had an idea. Tom Sawyer had once tricked his Aunt Polly when she'd cornered him. He'd done something to make her look away for just a minute. Would the same trick work now? She had to try it. It was her only chance.

"Look! A rat! Get it, Tom, get it!"

Ruby screamed. Then she turned to look at the cat. The minute Ruby looked away, Beth ran into the kitchen, out the back door, and down the steps.

Beth was in the middle of the backyard when she heard the shot. She dropped to the ground.

Beth looked over her shoulder. Ruby was standing at the top of the steps. She had an ugly look on her face. Ruby was pointing the gun right at Beth. This was it. This time Ruby would kill her.

Suddenly Beth heard the wail of a siren. It was the sheriff! Beth had never in her life been so happy to hear a siren.

Ruby gave an angry cry and turned to run into the house. Beth knew Ruby would grab the box and be gone in a minute. In the dark it might be hard to find her. It looked as if she were going to get away.

But Beth and Ruby had not counted on Tom. Just as Ruby turned to run back into the house, Tom shot out through the door. He was going so fast that he ran right into Ruby. Ruby tripped over him and fell down the steps. The gun flew out of her hand.

Beth jumped to her feet and ran to get the gun. She was holding it on Ruby when the sheriff got there.

"Beth, are you all right?"

Beth turned to see her neighbor walking toward her. Lila looked frightened. Beth gave the gun to the sheriff and put her arms around Lila.

The sheriff put his handcuffs on Ruby.

"I'm fine," Beth said. "Were you the one who called the sheriff?"

Lila nodded. "I was bringing that key over when I heard Ruby talking. I looked in the window and saw that she had a gun. I went back to my house and called the sheriff. Was she the one who broke in?"

Beth nodded. "Yes, and she almost killed me. Lila, you saved my life. You and Tom!"

"Tom?" Lila asked.

Beth told Lila and the sheriff the whole story. When she got to the part about Tom tripping Ruby, everyone but Ruby laughed.

"That's some cat you've got there, Miss Calloway," the sheriff said.

"Let's go see what's in the box," Beth said.

They all went into the house. Beth picked up the box and put it on the table. She took the small key from Lila and put it in the lock. The key fit.

Inside the box was a pile of handwritten pages that had gone yellow with age. Beth picked up the sheet on top. She began to read it slowly. Then she gasped.

"What is it?" Lila said.

"It's a story by Mark Twain!" Beth said. "A story he wrote for Sarah Evans when she was a little girl. He gave it to her as a gift. This was Sarah's secret."

"Which story is it?" Lila asked.

"You don't understand," Beth said. "This story has never been published!"

"I don't know much about these things," the sheriff said. "But I guess it might be pretty valuable."

"That's right," Beth said. "After all, Mark Twain is world famous."

"Oh, Beth, what are you going to do with it?" Lila asked.

"I'm not sure," Beth said. "I suppose I could sell it."

"You'll be rich," Lila said. "I guess you won't want to stay in Stony Creek now."

"Oh, I don't know if I'll be rich," Beth laughed. "But I can tell you one thing. I've been crazy with fear lately and I'm afraid I haven't treated people too kindly. I hope everyone will let me try again. Stony Creek's a nice town. I think I'd like to stay on."

"I think the people of Stony Creek would like to have you," the sheriff said.

"Yes," said Lila. "We would."